BIRD

Douglas Bender

TABLE OF CONTENTS

A Pelican Book

Teaching Tips for Caregivers and Teachers:

Research shows that one of the best ways for students to learn a new topic is to read about it.

Before Reading

- Read the title and predict what the book will be about.
- Read the "Words to Know" and discuss the meaning of each word.
- Read the back cover to see what the book is about.

During Reading

- When a student gets to a word that is unknown, ask them to look at the rest of the sentence to find clues to help with the meaning of the unknown word.
- Motivate students with praise and encouragement.

After Reading

- Discuss the main idea of the book.
- Ask students to give one detail that they learned in the book.

SIGHT WORDS

a
all
can
eat
fly
have
is
some
this

WORDS TO KNOW

bird

birdseed

cage

feathers

squawk

This is a **bird**.

bird

All birds can fly!

All birds have **feathers**.

feathers

Some birds have a **cage**.

cage

Some birds eat **birdseed**.

birdseed

All birds can **squawk**!

squawk

INDEX

Written by: Douglas Bender
Design by: Under the Oaks Media
Series Development: James Earley
Editor: Kim Thompson

Photos: Eric Isaelee: cover; Bored Photography: p. 5; Valentin Valkov: p. 7; tuthelens: p. 9; Shivrohit: p. 11; Sarychev Olesia: p. 13; Ritu Manoj Jethani: p. 15

Library of Congress PCN Data
Bird / Douglas Bender
My First Pet
ISBN 978-1-63897-432-1(hard cover)
ISBN 978-1-63897-547-2(paperback)
ISBN 978-1-63897-662-2(EPUB)
ISBN 978-1-63897-777-3(eBook)
Library of Congress Control Number: 2022932422

Printed in the United States of America.

Seahorse Publishing Company
www.seahorsepub.com

Published in the United States
Seahorse Publishing
PO Box 771325
Coral Springs, FL 33077